ART & CRAFT of WRITING
STORIES

SECOND WRITER'S MANUAL

LA
FAVORITA
PRESS

Mendocino, California

victoriamixon.com

Published by La Favorita Press
PO Box 1203, Mendocino, CA 95460
lafavoritapress.com

ISBN 978-1-944227-02-9

Text set in Book Antiqua, by Monotype Staff, Microsoft Typography. Titles and headings set in Poor Richard, by Keystone Type Foundry.

Art & Craft of Writing Fiction™, La Favorita Press™, and the La Favorita graphic are trademarks of La Favorita Press. All other trademarks are trademarks of their respective owners.

Manufactured in the United States of America

Art & Craft of Writing

Sign up to get your
free books on writing!

artandcraftofwriting.com/freebooks

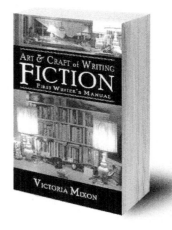

Acknowledgements

Again—I am so deeply grateful to all my editing clients and blog and magazine/laboratory readers, who surreptitiously contributed to the book. When I need someone to write to and for, you are there. I'm very grateful to Lucia Orth for her kind and meticulous help and to Jon Green for wonderful conversation. And I am of course eternally grateful to my husband, who does everything around here except write my books for me, and my son, who is the light of my life and the joy of my heart, the real motivation behind everything I do.

Table of Contents

PLOT IS CONTEXT

PART 2: REVISION

CONCLUSION

The State of the Industry

Fiction

One day last year some of us were talking about work habits — whether or not it's essential to write every single day, how to prioritize writing projects, whether or not to quantify output or time, what's the best way to start writing each time.

And the answers all came down to one thing:

Why are we writing our stories?

Maybe we're writing them because we grew up in the 1950s and '60s and '70s reading books by authors who — even though they weren't famous — still made a sort of lower-middle-class living staying home with a typewriter all day doing what they were good at and loved. And that was the future we saw for ourselves. Because we just love books.

Or maybe we're writing because, even though we've never been writers before, these stories have come to us, and we really, seriously, passionately want to tell them, but the more we work on them the more we want to tell them *exactly right*. And so we're struggling to learn how to discover exactly the right way.

Or maybe we're writing to become the next J.K. Rowling and make history in the industry and become famous as that break-out success everyone's still talking about twenty years later. Truth be told, when we think this way we probably aren't thinking about twenty years from now. We're probably only thinking about next year and whether or not we'll be so excited that we'll vomit on Oprah.

Or maybe we're writing because everywhere we go these days people are asking us if we're on Twitter and Facebook, whether or not we have blogs, if we have a 'social media following' out there 'online.' And when we *do* go online everywhere we look people are talking about how we have to start marketing our books before we even write them, and they're critiquing each other's manuscripts and offering for critique their own manuscripts on forums, and they're bemoaning their wordcounts and trading tips on blogging agents and asking us if we're doing NaNoWriMo this year.

And as soon as we ask ourselves, "Am I? Why not?" we realize that we've opened the Pandora's Box of writing advice that hammers at us relentlessly from all directions.

"Build your platform! Drive your traffic! Leverage your network! Accumulate your subscribers!"

As though the whole world were out there right this second waiting around just for *us* — for us to give it what *it wants* — and none too patiently either.

And we're thinking, *Huh. I always thought I was supposed to learn how to write well before I could sell anything that I'd written. How wrong was I?. . .*

Now, more than ever in history, the aspiring writer must guard against other people's agendas. We must consider every day with as much clarity and self-awareness as we can muster why we, personally, write. We must ask ourselves why we write *what* we write, just what we want to get out of writing, and how badly we want to get it.

We must ask every single time we sit down with our stories, "Why this? Why me? Why now?"

We must keep our heads when all those around us are losing theirs.

Because the world of illusion has finally come off the page and taken over the actual experience of being a writer. It can seem it's no longer about getting into that page and sinking with luxurious, tactile pleasure through the layers and layers and layers of brilliant and significant and riveting detail to the core underlying everything we could ever hope to write. As though it's no longer about climbing back out of those depths when we look up and around and realize we're sitting in a chair, at a desk, in a room, at a window, and our lives are here with us. No longer about going downstairs to sit on the front steps in the twilight after a solid day's work and think of those satisfying pages, smell the grass, listen to the birds, watch the clouds cross the iridescent sky, feel the good, firm earth beneath our bare feet.

It's all Barnum & Bailey now, scattered into the virtual blogosphere twenty-four hours a day, seven days a week, always and forever unto infinity.

We must remember, as we live our lives — this life of the writer in the twenty-first century — what an illusion the circus is. And remember what they say is born every minute.

We didn't choose this craft to be the craft of our souls just so we could be *that*.

We must turn our backs on the circus.

We must turn to our stories.

Part 1

Storytelling

Chapter 1

Loving in the Time of Cholera with Gabriel Garcia Marquez

Storytelling for the ages

I have a wonderful writer friend whom I love to death, but he has dyslexia like nobody's business, plus he doesn't think of himself as an intellectual. He's great if one of you has to climb a drainpipe to break into an upstairs apartment in the middle of a blistering hot summer afternoon. *Ask me how I know.* (He said, "Bring my keys." He did *not* say, "Don't bring one of those extra sets of car keys that my roommate leaves lying around everywhere.")

And he's actually quite an imaginative writer, because his dyslexia forces him to be certain that every single word he puts down he really *needs* to put down. Years ago, when we were young and intense and tragically-hip, I used to type his poetry for him. He'd lean over my shoulder in his ratty San Francisco apartment on lower Haight Street (where the dealers and druggies were even worse than in my neighborhood in the upper Tenderloin), watching me disentangle 'cigarette' from the extra y's and z's that he'd given it and laughing.

"So *that's* how you spell that!"

But it took him two years to read Gabriel Garcia Marquez' *One Hundred Years of Solitude*, carrying it everywhere with him all day long every day. By the time he was done, it was as though he'd won the Olympics. I seriously thought it might take him. . .one hundred years. . .of solitude. . .

Because there is only one thing that's going to inspire a severely dyslexic non-intellectual to get all the way through *One Hundred Years of Solitude*.

And that's stunning craft.

Marquez is a craftsperson of infinitely fine sensibility. We could talk for hours (perhaps I will) about how he gets away with writing entire 400-page novels of one paragraph about characters all with the same name. It's a miracle.

But where he really clobbers us with his talent is in his endings.

Do you know why *Love in the Time of Cholera* is named that?

Because the final scene could only be orchestrated 1) between people in love, and 2) during a time of cholera.

Or what about Mario Vargas Llosa's *Aunt Julia and the Scriptwriter*? What kind of madman comes up with a love story that revolves around a 1950s radio soap opera producer (*not* one of the lovers) whose single marketing mechanism is personally insulting a random handful of people? Complete with a rat eating something nobody should ever talk about a rat eating? I read that book as a very young adult and was blown backward against the wall by the manic glee of Llosa's literary *chutzpah*.

If we can learn anything from these pillars of twentieth-century South American literature, it is that storytelling is (or was recently, anyway) alive and thriving in parts of the world with low literacy rates.

Why do you suppose that is?

Now I'm going to do something unpopular here, and that is take a swipe at Khaled Hosseini's *The Kite Runner*.

The Kite Runner had me completely engrossed for fully half the novel. It was gripping, it was detailed, it was powerful, it was real. The protagonist walks a fine line between wealthy Afghani political power and poor oppressed masses. Sometimes he stays on it. Sometimes he falls off. The details of his struggle are beautiful, harsh, believable. He's *human*.

Then he and his father finally make it to the U.S. I always start to lose interest when characters with fascinatingly different experiences wind up living boring mainstream American lives, but I was rolling with that, rolling with the exploration of how the loss of their wealth and political power affected them, because up until there it had all been so true.

Then he grows up and goes back.

And this should have been the heart of the novel, everything a Climax is meant to be. We should have gotten to go into this character's childhood culture — which we have some real identification with now, because of that lush first half of the novel — and lived the internal drama of what happens on atmospheric re-entry. What happens when you put a human being through that. What happens to their insides.

Instead, we get a bizarre new plotline about hunting down a child through the evil tyranny of the Taliban and adopting it.

Heh? A new character? This late in the book? Someone we're supposed to bond to and feel enormous investment in? Someone we don't know anything about except second-hand through another character's version of what's happened? Someone so important that we're willing to drop the whole exploration of human experience we've been caught up in *until this point* and suddenly veer off into a completely different plot involving the child of a character we *might* feel bonded to based upon that lush build-up, except that he's never put in an appearance, and a situation that *might* matter to us if we'd had any idea such a thing could eventually happen?

Suddenly it's all violence and mayhem, the writer telling us what to think and how to feel about the Taliban, a totally different story from the long, meticulous accumulation of character and atmosphere of the earlier part of the book.

People, don't do this to yourself. Don't force the awareness of your literary limitations on your reader by ignoring the true story you have chosen to tell.

Read *Love in the Time of Cholera* and study the plot and style. Marquez is very clear from the outset: this is not memoir, this is fiction. Fermina and Florentino spend the entire novel spanning the years of their lives at a distance, their youthful love long lost in the myriad of nuances that make up the profound truth about life lived out over decades. Watch how Marquez builds the plot points with subtle, unerring care. Sink up to your eyeballs in the wonderful plethora of telling detail and characterization, the gradual, sure-handed building of inevitable tension.

Then read the pen-penultimate page about the armed patrol on the river guarding against pestilence.

Three hundred and fifty pages—and the answer to one simple question is where this story was going *all along*.

Chapter 2

Searching for Entertainment-Industry Intelligence

A crash course

My husband and I fell in love under the shadow of SETI.

SETI, in case you don't know, stands for Search for Extra-Terrestrial Intelligence. When one morning almost twenty years ago my new boss (and future husband) pointed out that the company we worked for was right down the hall from the SETI offices, I laughed out loud. I didn't know you could *rent office space* in Silicon Valley from which to search for ET.

But as it happens, SETI, in spite of its *X Files*-type mission, enjoys a serious reputation among scientists and serves as a funding clearinghouse for a great deal of astronomical research, with enormous grants from some very highly-placed institutions indeed.

All this is by way of explaining where I spent a certain weekend one summer.

My husband had spent the week right before that in Boston leading seminars at one of the major Linux conferences, where he was approached by the SETI people to attend their first annual conference. He was one of a handful of open-source advocates invited to be involved in a discussion on moving

SETI's software to open source. He was also invited to their black-tie gala, at which astronauts, Star Trek stars, and big names in astronomy got up and talked about the future of space exploration. They were holding this conference at a large hotel in Silicon Valley, only a few hours' drive from where we live. So we went. Of course!

But the really important part of the conference came the day after the black-tie gala, when we attended a talk by the Director of the National Academy of Sciences' Science & Entertainment Exchange on the question: *How can we better bridge the gap between science-fiction entertainment and science?*

We watched a wonderful pastiche of movie clips to illustrate this intriguing question, and afterward the Director of the Science & Entertainment Exchange spoke long and eloquently. She brought up several points that, in my mind, all fit into the puzzle the same way:

- Laypeople learn "science" from sci-fi entertainment
- Using science in sci-fi entertainment *significantly influences* the behavior of 'consumers' (a sitcom featuring science about breast cancer resulted in a major increase in women across the country getting check-ups, while a sitcom based on forensic science resulted in a four-fold increase in enrollment in forensic studies programs)
- The difference between a hacker staring at a screen for twenty seconds and then yelping, "Eureka!" is a far cry from the real hacker who stares at a screen for weeks on end before unraveling the complexities in their way
- The stories of scientists and their search for information often make gripping telling
- *It's more interesting to know the truth*

She explained that the National Academy of Sciences consults, when asked, on sci-fi movies and TV shows (which is where this Director's job comes in). They also, when not asked to consult, stand by watching the ensuing confusion.

"What can we do about this disconnect?" The Director of the Science & Entertainment Exchange asked.

She described the elitism among scientists that keeps them from being interested in fiction, the lack of understanding among many writers that science-fiction must be based on— who knew?—science. She even told us about her scientist husband's attempt to write a screenplay on what he knows about the potential and lack of potential in time travel, outraged by the ignorance displayed in time-travel sci-fi. ("This is really hard!" he finally said.)

She proposed a Writing Workshop in which writers and scientists would be paired off, so the scientists could keep the writers in the real world while they developed their stories.

And she mentioned that Steven Spielberg was in talks with her friend, the theoretical physicist Kip Thorne. (These talks eventually resulted years later in the brilliant movie *Interstellar*, co-produced by Thorne and based upon the real theoretical science of cosmology and time travel.)

Fabulous! I thought, *This all makes perfect sense.*

Because the truth is that a storyteller is dependent upon the facts of the reality they share with their reader—the hidden life-&-death struggles controlling all human character, the cause-&-effect of events in a temporal world, the meticulous, sensitive selection and accumulation of real details—to create a reflection of life that, when gazed into, resonates with a profundity that's always present in reality but often missed.

Storytelling is not something that interferes with life. It's not about faking or trivializing reality for the sake of the writer.

Storytelling is about waking the reader up to the life that's *really there*.

We must look for true aspects of character that we find utterly riveting. Explore real needs that power enormous agendas. Find ways to embed in these riveting characters with these powerful needs the counter-needs that create, deep inside them, internal conflict that rings inside the reader with devastating recognition.

"I *know* this person," the reader thinks. "With all their beauty and horror, their insight and idiocy, their innocence and corruption. *This person is me!*"

Then we give our characters some fascinating premise. What if ionizing the air could bend lightwaves to alter the paths of lasers? (An example of true science from the Director's talk.) What if time machines were possible, but altering the past through time travel were not? (Another example.) What if ghosts were the vibrations of the subatomic 'strings' that once made up the body of the living, continuing to reverberate after the body is gone? (I made up that one.)

What kind of nightmare could this create?

We put our characters into that nightmare.

And we design a plotline—along the lines of classic structure—around deeper and deeper exploration of the detailed, concrete reality that not only makes this nightmare possible but contains the *only conceivable antidote*.

We illuminate with words the eloquent search for truth that drives us all.